D1467984

SPOTLIGHT
ON CHILDREN'S
AUTHORS

GAIL CARSON LEVINE

LAURA L. SULLIVAN

Cavendish
Square

New York

Published in 2015 by Cavendish Square Publishing, LLC
243 5th Avenue, Suite 136, New York, NY 10016

Copyright © 2015 by Cavendish Square Publishing, LLC

First Edition

No part of this publication may be reproduced, stored in a retrieval system, or transmitted in any form or by any means—electronic, mechanical, photocopying, recording, or otherwise—without the prior permission of the copyright owner. Request for permission should be addressed to Permissions, Cavendish Square Publishing, 243 5th Avenue, Suite 136, New York, NY 10016. Tel (877) 980-4450; fax (877) 980-4454.

Website: cavendishsq.com

This publication represents the opinions and views of the author based on his or her personal experience, knowledge, and research. The information in this book serves as a general guide only. The author and publisher have used their best efforts in preparing this book and disclaim liability rising directly or indirectly from the use and application of this book.

CPSIA Compliance Information: Batch #WS14CSQ

All websites were available and accurate when this book was sent to press.

Library of Congress Cataloging-in-Publication Data

Sullivan, Laura L., 1974-
Gail Carson Levine / Laura L. Sullivan.
pages cm. — (Spotlight on children's authors)
Includes index.
ISBN 978-1-62712-852-0 (hardcover) — ISBN 978-1-62712-853-7 (paperback) ISBN 978-1-62712-854-4 (ebook)
1. Levine, Gail Carson—Juvenile literature. 2. Authors, American—20th century—Biography—Juvenile literature.
3. Children's stories—Authorship—Juvenile literature. I. Title.

PS3562.E8965Z84 2014
813'.54—dc23
[B]

2014002016

Editorial Director: Dean Miller
Editor: Andrew Coddington
Copy Editor: Cynthia Roby
Art Director: Jeffrey Talbot

Designer: Amy Greenan
Production Manager: Jennifer Ryder-Talbot
Production Editor: David McNamara
Photo Researcher by J8 Media

The photographs in this book are used by permission and through the courtesy of: Cover, Mark Mainz/Getty Images; Courtesy David Levine, 4, 9, 14-15, 21, 22, 33, 34, 37, 39; Michael S. Yamashita/National Geographic/Getty Images, 6; Urbano Delvalle/TIME & LIFE Pictures/Getty Images, 10; Society of Children's Book Writers and Illustrators (SCBWI), 12; DAVID APPLEBY/KRT/Newscom, 16; Evan Agostini/Getty Images, 19; Mary Evans Picture Library Ltd/age fotostock, 27; North Wind Picture Archives/The Image Works, 28; Feature Photo Service/Newscom, 29; Bloomberg/Getty Images, 30.

Printed in the United States of America

CONTENTS

INTRODUCTION:

Climbing the Danger Rocks

Along the west side of the lower Hudson River in northeastern New Jersey and southern New York rise a line of steep cliffs known as the Palisades. Several spurs of this incredible rock formation jut upward in a park right across the street from renowned author Gail Carson Levine's childhood home. She called them the "Danger Rocks." Though the intimidating, steep rocks seemed impossible to climb, Gail gritted her teeth and never gave up: "Going up, clinging to the cracks with my fingertips, terrified, I'd think, *if I live, I will never do this again*. When I reached the top I'd work my way down and start over just as frightened as before." It was that determination against the odds, against her own fear, that helped make Gail one of today's favorite children's authors.

From the outside, Gail's story appears to be a rocket to instant success. Her debut novel, *Ella Enchanted*, won a Newbery Honor and was soon grabbed by Hollywood and made into a hit movie. Even so, one of Gail's early submissions elicited this critique from an editor: "*Sweet Fanopps* is an example of a story which in my opinion does not have enough of a plot. The idea is very basic and it's not very emotionally charged … I don't think it has enough substance to be successful."

For nine years Gail sent out queries. It seemed as if every editor in the publishing world responded with a rejection letter. Nevertheless, she never gave up. Then, like the fairy tales Gail writes, her dreams suddenly came true.

Gail spent many happy days exploring
The Cloisters, a museum near her childhood
home dedicated to medieval art.

Chapter 1

HIDING IN THE BATHROOM

Gail grew up in the Washington Heights neighborhood of New York City. It was the 1950s, a time very much shaped by the aftermath of World War II. In her diverse neighborhood lived many families who had fled from Hitler's horrors, and German was as widely spoken as English on her block. Gail lived right across the street from her elementary school, P.S. 173, and J. Hood Wright Park (home of the "Danger Rocks").

The world felt as if it was a safer place then, and Gail had the run of the city. Three museums were in easy walking distance from her home. These included The Cloisters, which is constructed from pieces of original European abbeys carried across the ocean, and houses exhibits of medieval art.

At age eleven, Gail was allowed to ride the subway alone, so all of New York City was hers to explore. During the summer she could take a two-hour subway ride to the beach and stay there all day. In the winter she ice skated in Central Park. She needed the freedom that the big city offered because at home her family lived in relatively cramped conditions. Gail had to share a bedroom with her sister, who is five years her senior. They didn't get along very well back then, and Gail felt as if she had no privacy. (Gail is very close to her sister now that they're adults. Rani Carson is a painter who works in Jamaica.) She discovered solitude in her own personal haven of books. "No one could join me in a book, no one could comment on the action or make fun of it," Gail has said. She would lock herself in the bathroom and read for hours on end—which made some trouble in the household, because the family only had one bathroom.

Gail read every book she could get her hands on. In fact, most of her allowance went toward library fines for overdue books. She also wrote stories, painted, and acted. Yet reading remained special. Even today, Gail says, "There's still nothing as private as a book!"

Despite being an avid reader and writer of stories during her childhood, Gail never imagined that she would one day become an author. Instead, she dreamed of being an actress or an artist. She gave up on the idea of acting at a fairly young age, but her hopes of an artistic career persisted. Despite working hard, she was never satisfied with her creations. When she drew and painted, she always seemed to hear a voice inside her head telling her that she wasn't good enough.

It was when Gail was an adult and already well established in another career that she took a class in writing and illustrating for children. She discovered how much she loved the writing—but didn't really care about the illustration side after all. When she wrote, she found that the critical voice in her head fell silent.

That voice, she said, had been the enemy of her creativity. "I think lots of people hear a voice like that," Gail said, "and we all have to learn to tell it to shut up!"

Gail attended first Antioch College in Ohio, then City College of New York, where she was a member of the Phi Beta Kappa society—one of the most prestigious honor societies—and earned a Bachelor's Degree in Philosophy. She also met and married her husband, David Levine, a noted photographer, jazz pianist, and all-around witty guy.

Like many writers, Gail held other jobs during her life. For twenty-seven years she held government jobs for the State of New York. It was toward the middle of that career that Gail was tasked to write promotional materials for the New York Department of Commerce. That helped her get in the swing of writing every day, and she soon began seriously writing fiction.

Gail and her husband, David.

WHAT'S IN A NAME?

Gail's married name is "Levine" (pronounced Le-VEEN, rhymes with green). Yet she also uses her maiden name, Carson, for her books. She'd hoped that childhood friends who only knew her by Carson would find her when her books were published—and they did!

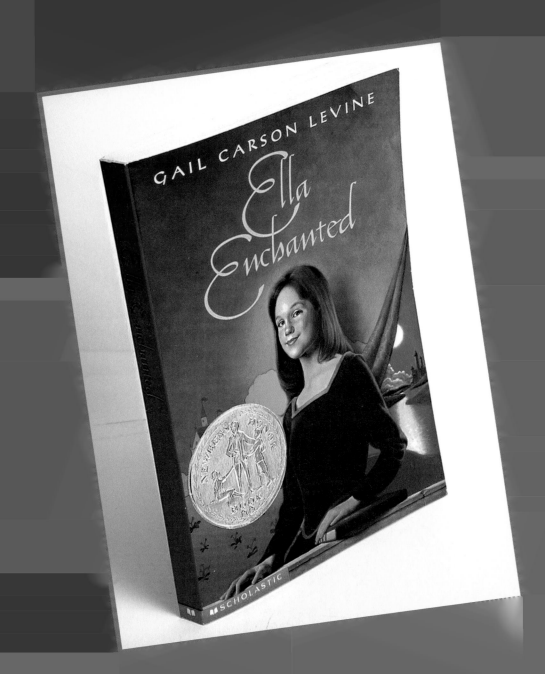

Chapter 2
NINE YEARS LATER...

Gail's first serious attempt at writing for children was in the 1970s when she wrote the script for *Spacenapped*, a musical performed by a Brooklyn community theater. Her husband, David, wrote the music and lyrics. She still didn't consider herself a "real writer," however. Then one day, while meditating, Gail says a stray thought came into her head: "I asked myself why, since I adored stories, I never made any up."

Inspired, she began to work on her first book for children, *The King's Cure,* an art appreciation book. Gail created some of the illustrations herself—those early plans to be an artist came in handy. She also planned to use reproductions of famous artwork to complement her story. Although it was never published, the effort convinced Gail to devote herself to writing for children.

She planned out her new goal systematically and seriously, doing all of the things that she currently recommends to budding writers. This included taking writing classes and joining critique groups to share her work with other aspiring writers. She also became a member of the Society of Children's Book Writers and Illustrators,

society of children's book writers & illustrators

Many writers, including Gail, recommend that aspiring children's authors join the Society for Children's Book Writers and Illustrators (SCBWI).

an international organization that supports the creation of books for young people and offers education and support for its members.

Early in her career, Gail focused on creating picture books. She sent them to many editors and publishers but was rejected every time. Some of the rejections hurt. She was told that her picture books lacked strong plots, well-developed characters, or depth of emotion. Some editors just responded with generic form letters, so Gail never knew whether or not they had read her books. Others, though, were more helpful, mailing kind little notes or specific comments about her writing. "Some of the rejections were actually quite encouraging," Gail said. She learned from the rejections and continued to submit.

Despite being unpublished, it was a happy time for Gail. Instructors and the other students in her writing classes and critique groups were very supportive of her work. Best of all, Gail was improving her writing every day, honing her craft.

Nine years later, Gail was in a new writing class and searching for ideas. She'd just read Robin McKinley's *Beauty*, which is a retelling of the traditional *Beauty and the Beast* tale. This inspired her to try a new take on a fairy tale, too. The classic story *Cinderella* was the one that came immediately to mind. The only problem was that Gail realized she didn't really like or respect the main character. Cinderella, she felt, is too good, too willing to obey her cruel, overbearing stepsisters.

It took a leap of imagination to figure out a way to write about a character she found annoying. "I was in trouble until I thought of the curse of obedience," Gail said. "Then I got it. Ella has to do as she's told, and she takes revenge whenever she can." The character Ella wasn't a goody-goody or a pushover—she was under a curse. Once Gail understood the nature of her heroine, she was able to write her first full-length novel, *Ella Enchanted*. Confident in her work, she began to submit the manuscript.

Then, it finally happened—not one but two acquisition editors wanted to buy *Ella Enchanted*. On April 17, 1996, she sold her first manuscript to HarperCollins. Gail describes it as one of the happiest days of her life. Her professional writing career had officially begun.

Then, to her surprise, *Ella Enchanted* received one of the top awards in children's literature: a Newbery Honor. Being awarded that honor had more influence on Gail's life than on her writing. "It offered me many opportunities to travel to schools and conferences," she said. "It made me known, so now there's an audience for my other books, even when they don't also win such terrific recognition. That's the biggest effect, and the most wonderful."

In fairy tales, things tend to happen in threes. The first was publication, then second, earning a major award. Gail had no idea that the "magical third" was just around the corner.

Gail Carson Levine always reaches for her dreams.

Anne Hathaway played the part of Ella in the movie version of *Ella Enchanted*, while Hugh Dancy played the part of Prince Char.

Chapter 3
ELLA GOES TO HOLLYWOOD

In the third magical aspect of Gail's fairy-tale rise to success, Hollywood called on her with an option in hand. An option is the first step in turning a book into a movie. When a producer, production company, or studio has their eye on a novel, they usually don't immediately buy the right to make it into a movie. Instead, they option it—in place of an outright purchase, they simply secure the right to be the only one to buy it in the future. Hollywood sometimes moves even more slowly than the publishing industry, so options can be repeatedly renewed before the movie goes into production. Unfortunately, sometimes the movie never gets made at all. When *Ella Enchanted* was optioned, Gail wasn't holding her breath.

When Gail was given the news that Ella was definitely going to be a movie, she could hardly believe it. "I thought [Ella] might sell a few thousand copies and go out of print," she said. "I still pinch myself over the way things have worked out."

As the movie-making process progressed, Gail discovered that an author doesn't always have that much say regarding exactly how her book is adapted into a film script. The terms of her contract ensured that she'd have consulting rights—that she'd get to read the script and offer comments—but there was no guarantee that they'd heed any of her opinions. "When I saw the script, I wasn't happy about the addition of an evil uncle and a talking snake," Gail said. "Those comments were ignored."

Gail's ideas about plot changes weren't at all considered, but her thoughts about employing the plot device of obedience certainly were. In the story, baby Ella is given a "gift" by the fairy Lucinda— she has to obey any command that anyone gives her. She tries to keep it a secret so people won't take advantage of her. After Ella's mother dies, however, her new stepfamily figures out the "gift" and makes her life miserable. Ella begins a quest to break the curse (and finds true love along the way). It was very important to Gail that the moviemakers respect the central idea of Ella's forced obedience.

"I said there had to be consistency in the way Ella responds to orders," Gail said. "She could follow commands figuratively or literally, but it needed to be the same throughout. In my book, Ella follows the meaning of commands. If she were told to hold her tongue, she'd be silent." But the movie took a much more literal, and visually hilarious approach to Ella's obedience. "In the movie, Anne Hathaway [the actress playing Ella] actually grabs her tongue and holds it."

Anne Hathaway's acting "chops," or ability, impressed Gail. Hathaway could run the same line a hundred different ways, incorporating subtle changes each time. She would do this until she got it exactly right. A mime was brought in to help the actress perfect Ella's body language. Since Ella is under the power of a curse, her mind might want to do one thing, while her body is forced to do another. The professional mime taught Hathaway how to make Ella's body appear to respond involuntarily to any command, even while Ella's mind was rebelling against it.

"I like the movie," Gail said. "Anne Hathaway is the perfect Ella." All the same, she cautions that the book and movie are very

Lucinda (played by Vivica A. Fox in the movie version) is the bungling fairy whose gifts are actually curses in *Ella Enchanted.*

ANNE HATHAWAY WAS A NATURAL ELLA

Ella Enchanted star Anne Hathaway seemed to have a personal connection to Gail. Since her character in the film has such trouble from a fairy godmother, someone asked her if she had a godmother of her own. She replied, "I do have a godmother in real life, and she's a bit small and petite and looks a bit like Gail Carson Levine."

Anne Hathaway also said that she really wanted to do the movie because she loved the book. "I just thought it was such a wonderful project. Gail's characters are so great... I just want to write children's books for the rest of my life and have that lovely life."

different and should be considered as entirely separate creations. Each, she thinks, can be enjoyed on its own terms. Some fans might be disappointed that the movie is different from the book. The book could have been followed exactly, Gail said, but that would have been a different—and not necessarily better—movie. What works on paper doesn't always work on the screen.

All the same, it was a fascinating experience for the author, and one that helped propel her career to even more stellar heights. When the movie was released, the studio toured Gail all over the

Gail (pictured with the stars of
Ella Enchanted) spent a few days on
the set while the movie was being filmed.

United States and Canada, which brought a lot of attention to her and her writing. She walked the red carpet at the movie's premier along with the stars, and even got a little on-screen time of her own in the bonus features of the DVD release. "The movie brought tons of readers to my book," Gail said. The new audience that adored Ella soon fell in love with Gail's other novels, too.

Gail is a big fan of fairy tales... and her
readers are big fans of her fairy tales!

Chapter 4
THE FAIRY TALE CONTINUES

The majority of Gail's books retell traditional fairy tales that are hundreds of years old, yet Gail imparts twists and turns that make each one absolutely fresh. She began her writing career on the cusp of a new trend for fairy tale retellings—or maybe even helped start the trend.

Fairy tales, Gail says, are timeless. "Fairy tales deal in universals: love, jealousy, rage, fear, death, beauty, acceptance, good, evil, and probably more. They provide instant entry into these deep topics." Though the core of many fairy tales is disturbing, they are also perfectly formulated to give young people a glimpse into some of the most primal human feelings in an accessible way.

After *Ella Enchanted* hit the shelves to great acclaim, Gail wrote *The Fairy's Mistake*, a story based on the *Toads and Diamonds* fairy tale. In the original version, a foul-tempered widow has two daughters. The elder is cruel like her mother (and thus her favorite) while the younger daughter is sweet like her father. One day, while the younger daughter is at the well, an old woman asks her for a drink. When the girl politely gives her a cup of water, the old woman reveals herself to be a fairy and rewards the girl by making precious jewels tumble from her mouth whenever she speaks. Later, when the fairy asks the unkind sister for a drink, she refuses, and the fairy punishes her by making toads and snakes fall from her mouth when she talks. Furious that her favorite is punished, the mother banishes her youngest daughter to the forest, where of course she meets and marries a handsome prince. Eventually, even the mother is disgusted by all the toads and snakes, and also banishes her eldest daughter to the woods. She, unfortunately, doesn't find a prince—only starvation and death.

In her usual skeptical fashion, Gail thought there was "plenty wrong" with this tale. For one, neither toads nor diamonds would be very comfortable coming from a girl's mouth. For another, Gail realized that the handsome prince who marries the good girl couldn't really love her—he just wanted her jewels. So Gail found a way to turn the diamonds into a curse, and the toads into a blessing. Gail's fairies don't always get things right!

The Fairy's Mistake was originally conceived as a picture book. Before the success of *Ella Enchanted*, no publisher agreed to take on the project. But when Gail showed the manuscript to her editor, she suggested Gail flesh it out and turn it into a chapter book—and then write two more. The end result was compiled into *The Princess Tales Volume One*, which also included *The Princess Test* (a take on *The Princess and the Pea*) and *Princess Sonora and the Long Sleep* (a version of *Sleeping Beauty*.) "The request came at the perfect time," Gail said, "just as I was figuring out if I could quit my job to write full-time. I decided I could!"

With the liberty to devote all of her time to her writing, Gail took on a project that was especially near and dear to her heart: *Dave at Night*. It was a radical departure from her fairy tales of magic and princesses. All the same, *Dave at Night* is Gail's favorite book because it is based on her father's childhood. "His name was Dave, and he was an orphan," Gail said. "I don't know how old he was when he was sent to the Hebrew Orphan Asylum, but he may have been as young as six, and he stayed until he was sixteen."

Gail's father never talked about his time in the orphanage. Once, she showed him a picture of the building. "Yup, that's it," was all her father would say. Then he walked away. Gail could tell from his demeanor that he had been unhappy there. Yet the man she knew was happy and cheerful. After he died in 1986, Gail decided to fictionalize his story, giving him the happiness and escape he might not have really had. Like some of her other early works, *Dave at Night* began as a picture book and eventually became the richly nuanced historical novel it is today.

In *Dave at Night*, a boy is sent to the orphanage when his father dies and his stepmother and other relatives refuse to take him in. His only treasure is a carving of Noah's Ark that his father, a woodworker, made. When the cruel headmaster steals the carving, and then starves and beats all the boys, David plots his escape. He can get out of the orphanage easily enough, but refuses to leave for good until he can get his carving back. Meanwhile, on his nightly sojourns he meets a Jewish fortune teller who pretends to be his grandfather, and discovers the rich jazz scene of Harlem nightlife. His new friends on the outside might be able to rescue him. But as he grows more attached to the other orphans, he wonders if it might be better to help them than to save himself.

Always one to experiment, Gail's next book returned to the fantasy she loves but in a completely modern setting. *The Wish* brings to light the questionable importance of popularity in eighth grade. In the story, friendless Wilma does a favor for a mysterious old lady and gets a wish in return—only, she doesn't phrase her wish quite right. She wishes to be the most popular girl in her school, forgetting that she'll be graduating in three weeks and then turn back into her boring, unpopular old self.

Some might think that a story with a contemporary setting wouldn't require any real research in the way that a historical novel does. But Gail found herself doing almost as much research for *The Wish* as she'd done for *Dave at Night*. "I don't have kids, and I rarely watch TV, and it's been a long time since I was fourteen, so I had to research being an eighth grader," Gail said. She spent a day following an eighth grade class around and asked them a lot of questions.

Gail was never actually enrolled in eighth grade. She was in a special program that allowed her to skip that year. (But she said she went to kindergarten twice, so that made up for it.) Her sophomore year, however, was a miserable experience. That provided the basis for some of Wilma's feelings in *The Wish*, although Gail points out that the work is still 99.9 percent fiction.

Peter Pan by J. M. Barrie was one of Gail's favorite books when she was a child.

Gail continued her penchant for fantasy and made-up worlds with *The Two Princesses of Bamarre*, a tale of a coward finding courage during dark times. She then published *The Princess Tales Volume Two*. This most recent trio of stories includes *Cinderellis and the Glass Hill* (A Cinder Lad story), *For Biddle's Sake* (Gail's favorite of the Princess Tales, based on the little-known Puddocky story), and *The Fairy's Return* (based on *The Golden Goose*). Then Gail revisited the world she created in *Ella Enchanted* with *Fairest*, a twist on the story of Snow White. In *Fairest*, the bungling gift-giving fairy Lucinda makes another appearance.

It was around this time Gail was invited to work on a special project that was dear to her heart. When Gail was a little girl, there wasn't a huge selection of fantasy novels available for children. One of the few, and one of Gail's favorites, was J. M. Barrie's

GAIL'S FAIRY TALES AREN'T SO GRIMM

Gail writes modern fairy tales for today's children. She was raised on the darkness of the Brothers Grimm, but admits that parents "may no longer want to scare their children witless in order to teach them to obey (*Little Red Riding Hood*), or to be truthful (*The Boy Who Cried Wolf*), or not to lose themselves in rage and jealousy (*Snow White*)." Gail's books take on the same themes and present them in a way much more palatable to modern children—with a dash of zaniness and humor. Still, Gail says, "I'm glad my parents didn't keep the [traditional darker] fairy tales from me. My imagination is richer for them, and they connected me to the fundamental struggles we all face."

Gail with illustrator David Christiana at a book tour event.

classic *Peter Pan*. Imagine her surprise and delight when Disney approached her to write a book about Never Land fairies set in Peter Pan's world. "I fell in love with Peter," Gail said. "I decided Wendy was an idiot for leaving him, and I wished I could jump inside the book and make things right."

While Gail didn't quite get to fulfill her childhood fantasy of marrying Peter Pan, she did get to play in his world for a while. She started with her rival for Peter's affections, Tinker Bell, and expanded the fairy world to create a thriving pixie civilization with a host of fascinating characters. Her first book in the series was *Fairy Dust and the Quest for the Egg*, which Disney presented in a lavish, heavily illustrated edition that hearkened back to old-fashioned children's books. Two more titles followed: *Fairy Haven and the Quest for the Wand* and *Fairies and the Quest for Never Land*.

Gail Carson Levine

Newbery Honor Author of *Ella Enchanted*

fairest

Fairest, a retelling of the
Snow White story, gave Gail more
trouble than any other book.

Chapter 5
A WRITER'S WRITER

Gail takes the craft of writing very seriously. Despite her obvious successes, she continues to view herself as a student of writing. Writing is always a struggle for Gail—even if it is a labor of love.

Sometimes, having the right time and place to write can be an author's greatest struggle. Luckily, Gail says she can write almost anywhere. In fact, the first draft of *Ella Enchanted* was mostly written while Gail rode on a commuter train to and from the city. "The hardest part is the first draft," she said. "While I'm writing it, I feel like I'm in prison, in an iron cell with no windows or doors, and I have no ideas." Then, slowly, the ideas start to come. Gail has said that she doesn't consider herself a person who has many ideas—they only come to her after hours of effort.

Revisions are the bane of many writers' lives, but for Gail they are the best part. She really enjoys going back over the work that took a lot of effort to write and finding ways to make it better. Sometimes, though, the revisions don't go at all smoothly. If she's lucky, she can tell that there's a problem right away. "The tip-off for me [is] boredom," Gail said. "I [write] slower and slower.

This is usually how I know when my story is in trouble." This is not always the case with her writing, however.

Fairest required more work and creativity than any other book Gail had ever written. It took her four years, and the problems with it weren't immediately clear. After slogging through nearly the entire novel, she decided that the point of view wasn't quite right. The main character in her reinvented Snow White tale is in a coma when some of the action is taking place. At first she tried to write it from the point of view of a gnome, then the prince, and then in the third person, omniscient point of view. None of these techniques worked—each try took her another 300 pages of revisions to make that discovery. However, Gail was stubborn. She couldn't bear to waste all those years of writing, and she persisted until she found a plot device and point of view that worked.

Fairest might have been the hardest book to write, but every book gives Gail some difficulty. This places her in a unique position to sympathize with writers who also struggle with their art. Her blog is dedicated not to self-promotion but to helping writers hone their craft. With posts that include information from techniques of writing the basic plot and complementing dialogue, to sorting out more complex issues such as making a difficult character likable, Gail dives headlong into the nuances of novel writing.

One of the most incredibly responsive authors, many of her blog posts are entirely devoted to answering her readers' questions about writing. She also includes writing prompts to help inspire them.

Gail at her desk in her "cozy" office.

Gail has facilitated writing workshops for middle school students for many years. Seeing how the children write has helped her develop her own work—not so much in style but in attitude. "One of the things that has helped me a lot, and that kind of stunned me when I started teaching kids, is how they just leap into writing. I give the kids a writing prompt, and they just start. They don't agonize over it. I find this very freeing."

Inspired by the kids' responses to her instruction, Gail decided to write a book that teaches children how to write. She titled it *Writing Magic: Creating Stories That Fly*. This work has been heralded as one of the best children's guides to writing. In addition to the author's valuable advice, she includes many of the prompts that she employed while teaching middle school kids. "I love dreaming up prompts," Gail says, "and they're probably my favorite parts of the book."

Gail lives in a 200-year-old
farmhouse in Brewster, New York.

Chapter 6
AT HOME WITH GAIL CARSON LEVINE

Gail and her husband live in an old farmhouse. It was built in 1790 and has been lovingly maintained. Constructed of red-painted wood with white trim, Gail describes it as old-fashioned and cozy, with low ceilings and small windows. Despite its great age, Gail reports that the house doesn't have a single ghost.

The Levines are kept company by the couple's dog, an Airedale named Reggie. Gail says he has "more energy than a power plant," which is typical of the breed. She added: "He has a great sense of humor which expresses itself in mischief. Pleasing us is not his top priority, although if it happens by luck, he's glad. He's very sweet and loves every person and every dog."

One of the prizes of the property is an authentic outhouse. Although Gail assures people that there are actual working bathrooms inside their home, the outhouse in an interesting curiosity. It remained in use as late as 1945. During some recent repairs, Gail had the land underneath the outhouse excavated. The work uncovered mementos of past residents' lives, including old medicine bottles and a child's doll.

The landscape surrounding the Levine home is beautiful, boasting ancient maples and a very old apple tree. The garden is peaceful and filled with local wildlife—except when Reggie is chasing rabbits. Gail enjoys being outdoors in her own private paradise. Whenever she's stuck for an idea, she'll go outside and often discover one among the tranquility of nature.

Gail's workspace is on the second story in "the smallest, coziest room in this cozy house." It is sparsely furnished to avoid distractions, featuring only a desk, chair, two bookcases, and a bed, which she uses for meditation, not for sleeping. But there's still plenty of snoozing going on in the artwork in that room. Over her desk hang two drawings: one of a sleeping polar bear created by an illustrator friend, the other a picture of Gail sleeping when she was about six years old. It was drawn by her sister, Rani, who Gail describes as being immensely talented, even back then at age eleven.

Of course, Gail isn't just a writer. She has lots of hobbies, and does many things to help her relax. She has a passion for walking, both in her beautiful countryside, and in her old stomping ground, New York City. "I adore walking," Gail said. "I could walk forever. The rhythm that gets into me is pure pleasure." She also has a dedicated fitness regime. Gail lifts weights under the direction of a trainer and has developed some impressive muscles. "For a person who weighs about eighty-seven pounds, I'm very strong. I can bench press ninety pounds when I'm at my peak." For cardio, Gail blasts rock music in the basement and dances. Even though Gail is dedicated to her writing, she still finds that it is easy for life

Gail is very strong—
particularly for a woman
of her age and size.

to distract her from her work. "I can't resist looking at e-mails when they come in," Gail said. "I answer the phone when it rings." Luckily, she says she can work almost anywhere, and even multitask. "At home, I write while I eat breakfast, lunch, and my evening snack (ice cream or pie, and spearmint tea)."

All her time spent writing has led Gail to branch out with her art. She has taken on a new writing endeavor: poetry for adults. Switching from writing fiction for children to writing poetry for grown-ups, Gail says, "feels as if I step from one room in my brain to another… In my poetry room I'm less analytical and more relaxed than in my novel writing room." It is easier, in some ways, not to have to carry the weight of many characters and a long, complex plot. "I go into more of a trance when I write poetry. My mind settles."

Gail is currently pursuing a Master of Fine Arts (MFA) degree in Poetry at New York University. Now, she has to deal with occasional rejection all over again. Several magazines have turned down some of her adult poems, despite her famous name.

Gail is also in the early stages of a couple of new writing projects for kids. During her semester break, she'll be working on edits of her latest novel, *Stolen Magic*, which is a sequel to *A Tale of Two Castles*. She has even started writing the first few pages of a brand new novel, a prequel to *The Two Princesses of Bamarre,* but she admits she likely won't have much time to work on that until her summer vacation. Poetry will remain her primary focus for the time being.

She's not abandoning her fans who are budding writers, though. Soon she'll have another book to help them advance in their writing craft. Based on many of the questions and answers discussed on her blog, *Writer to Writer* is scheduled for release in early 2015.

Someone once asked Gail if she ever thought her life would turn out as it has: with bestselling books and a movie that has become a classic to her name. This was probably the only time her imagination ever failed her. She said, "I didn't have the imagination to think of everything that's happened. What's happened has been totally astonishing. Sometimes I think I'm going to wake up and tell my husband about this wonderful dream I've had."

Luckily for her fans, Gail is always
busy writing something. She's in
the writing life for *good*.

GAIL'S TIPS FOR YOUNG WRITERS

Stick to it and be patient.

"Patience and stubbornness are the two qualities a writer needs most."

Save and revise.

"Save everything you write. I think kids abandon stories all the time. They start stories and get frustrated or get a different, better idea. I think that it is more worthwhile to stick with a story and revise it and try to finish it than abandon ship. Revisions, for any writer, are the name of the game."

Be a joiner.

Some writers tend to keep their work in progress to themselves, but Gail thinks sharing with other writers can provide valuable insight.

Writers have to be readers.

"Read about writing," Gail says, adding, "and read the kind of books you are writing."

Don't go easy on your characters.

"For kids who are writing, make your characters suffer! If you're getting bored with a story, make something terrible happen to your main character." Gail thinks characters need the impetus of hardship to make them interesting. She makes characters orphans or gives them a curse, and voila, they suddenly have a need to take action.

And the most important lesson, gleaned from Gail's own life and struggles:

"Never give up!"

BOOKS BY GAIL CARSON LEVINE

Ella Enchanted (1997)

Dave at Night (1999)

The Wish (2000)

The Two Princesses of Bamarre (2001)

The Princess Tales: Volume 1 (2002)

Betsy Who Cried Wolf (2002)

The Princess Tales: Volume 2 (2004)

Fairy Dust and the Quest for the Egg (2005)

The Fairy's Return and Other Princess Tales (2005)

Fairest (2006)

Writing Magic: Creating Stories That Fly (2006)

Fairy Haven and the Quest for the Wand (2007)

Ever (2008)

Fairies and the Quest for Never Land (2010)

A Tale of Two Castles (2011)

Forgive Me, I Meant to Do It (2012)

GLOSSARY

editor—in general, a person who works to improve the quality of a piece of writing—an editor is usually the employee of a publishing company who first reads and then decides to buy an author's novel

fairy tale—short, often old or traditional stories that frequently deal with magic, enchantment, or mythical creatures, in which unlikely heroes or heroines find success through their wits or magical help; fairy tales often contain lessons or disguised morals

Newbery Medal—an award given each year for the best children's books—one book is selected to receive the medal, and up to five others are named Newbery Honor books

option—if a movie producer or film studio wants to turn a book into a movie, they first buy the right to be the only one allowed to officially buy the rights to the book within a certain time; because movie deals take a long time to close, the option is often renewed many times

prequel—a book or story set chronologically before an existing book; a book written in the historical past of an existing story

prompt—a suggested idea, question, or situation to give a writer inspiration; prompts are generally used for practice writing exercises

query—the letter an author sends to a literary agent or editor in the hopes of enticing them to read, and eventually represent or buy their book

revision—changing, correcting, or improving an early draft of a manuscript

third person omniscient—a point of view in a story in which all details about all characters are known and described by a narrator who is not directly involved in the action

CHRONOLOGY

September 17, 1947: Gail Carson Levine is born.

1964–1967: Gail attends Antioch College in Ohio.

1967: Gail marries David Levine, and transfers to City College of New York.

1969: Gail receives her Bachelor of Arts degree in Philosophy from City College of New York.

1987: Gail begins writing children's books in earnest.

1993: Gail and David purchase their 200-year-old farmhouse.

1996: *Ella Enchanted* is accepted for publication.

1997: *Ella Enchanted* is published.

1998: Gail receives a Newbery Honor for *Ella Enchanted*.

1999: *Dave at Night*, Gail's only historical novel, is published.

2004: *Ella Enchanted* the movie is released.

2005: Gail's first book in the Disney Fairies series is published.

2006: *Writing Magic: Creating Stories That Fly* is published, based on Gail's writing workshops with kids.

2012: Gail's first book of poetry for children, *Forgive Me, I Meant To Do It*, is published.

2013: Gail enrolls in New York University, pursuing her Master of Fine Arts degree in Poetry.

FURTHER INFORMATION

Books

Are you interested in writing your own stories? These three books can offer you guidance.

Fletcher, Ralph. *A Writer's Notebook: Unlocking the Writer Within You*. New York, NY. HarperCollins, 2003.

Levine, Gail Carson. *Writing Magic: Creating Stories that Fly*. New York, NY. HarperCollins, 2006.

Messner, Kate. *Real Revision: Authors' Strategies to Share with Student Writers*. Portland, ME. Stenhouse Publishers, 2011.

Websites

Gail Carson Levine's blog
gailcarsonlevine.blogspot.com

Gail Carson Levine's official website
www.gailcarsonlevine.com

The Society for Children's Book Writers and Illustrators
www.scbwi.org
You have to be over 18 to join, but you can still find helpful information on the site. It also includes the Blue Boards, one of the most helpful resources for children's writers on the Web.

BIBLIOGRAPHY

ONLINE SOURCES

"An Interview with Gail Carson Levine." Book Browse. www.bookbrowse.com/author_interviews/full/index.cfm/author_number/420/gail-carson-levine

"Gail Carson Levine." Harper Collins Author Interview. www.harpercollins.com/author/authorExtra.aspx?authorID=12385&displayType=interview

Gilchrist, Todd. "Ella Enchanted: An Interview with Anne Hathaway." April 2004, www.blackfilm.com/20040402/features/annehathaway.shtml

"Meet the Authors and Illustrators: Gail Carson Levine." RIF Reading Planet. www.rif.org/kids/readingplanet/bookzone/levine.htm

Smith, Cynthia Leitich. "Author Update: Gail Carson Levine." May 2, 2006, cynthialeitichsmith.blogspot.com/2006/05/author-update-gail-carson-levine.html

Smith, Cynthia Leitich. "Interview with Children's and YA Author Gail Carson Levine." December 2000, www.cynthialeitichsmith.com/lit_resources/authors/interviews/GailCarsonLevine.html

INDEX

ABOUT THE AUTHOR:

Laura L. Sullivan is a prolific author of books for middle grade and young adult readers. Her novels include the Under the Green Hill and Guardian of the Green Hill fantasy series, as well as the historical novels *Ladies in Waiting* and *Love by the Morning Star*. She lives on the west coast of Florida (and in a few fantasy worlds.) Her favorite Gail Carson Levine book is *Dave at Night*.